HOW TO LOSE WE

ON A MEDITERRANEAN DIET

Eva Evans

LEGAL & DISCLAIMER

The information contained in this book and its contents is not designed to replace or take the place of any form of medical or professional advice; and is not meant to replace the need for independent medical, financial, legal, or other professional advice or services, as may be required. The content and information in this book has been provided for educational and entertainment purposes only.

The content and information contained in this book has been compiled from sources deemed reliable, and it is accurate to the best of the Author's knowledge, information, and belief. However, the Author cannot guarantee its accuracy and validity and cannot be held liable for any errors and/or omissions. Further, changes are periodically made to this book as and when needed. Where appropriate and/or necessary, you must consult a professional (including but not limited to your doctor, attorney, financial advisor, or such other professional advisor) before using any of the suggested remedies, techniques, or information in this book.

Upon using the contents and information contained in this book, you agree to hold harmless the Author from and against any damages, costs, and expenses, including any legal fees potentially resulting from the application of any of the information provided by this book. This disclaimer applies to any loss, damages or injury caused by the use and application, whether directly or indirectly, of any advice or information presented, whether for breach of contract, tort, negligence, personal injury, criminal intent, or under any other cause of action. You agree to accept all risks of using the information presented inside this book.

You agree that by continuing to read this book, where appropriate and/or necessary, you shall consult a professional (including but not limited to your doctor, attorney, or financial advisor or such other advisor as needed) before using any of the suggested remedies, techniques, or information in this book.

TABLE OF CONTENT

INTRODUCTION

Eating healthy is one of the forms of self-love.

Have you ever wondered why people who live around the Mediterranean Sea are always in good shape, look happy, and enjoy their meals a little longer than anyone else?

Many people are not very fond of diets because they believe a diet is a temporary slimming method that is often a burden. On top of that, most diets are restrictive of delicious foods, which makes the whole slimming process quite challenging. But, have you wondered if there is a diet that could help you slim naturally while eating delicious meals? Most diets will cause the infamous yo-yo effect; once you stop following the diet and return to your old habits, your weight instantly returns.

Since the point here is losing weight and not returning to your old weight, I want to discuss with you one of the best eating patterns and lifestyles.

The Mediterranean Diet is an eating pattern that will help you make a healthy change in your eating habits without making you feel that you are restricting yourself from anything delicious.

You will enjoy your food and look forward to the next meal, because who wouldn't want to enjoy the Mediterranean tastes on a plate.

Rich in fruits and vegetables, healthy oils, delicious meals, and drinks, this diet will prove why it is so popular.

This diet will help you become more mindful of the foods you are consuming, how fresh they are, and what ingredients they contain.

Mindful eating is one of the most crucial steps towards becoming healthier, losing excess weight, and enjoying your balanced food.

This book's premise is to guide you through the process of beginning the Mediterranean diet's, learn about its benefits, carefully pick the suitable foods and drinks and slim healthily.

Let's get started!

HOW DOES MEDITERRANEAN DIET WORK?

Recognized by the UN as an endangered species, this diet, or rather an eating pattern, is based on the eating habits of rural people, who mainly ate what they grew. These people did not have the money to buy expensive foods (back in the days expensive food was meat), so they were mainly focused on eating the things they were able to pick from the ground and trees, or foods they were able to produce on their own such as pasta, oils, or catch in the sea (seafood).

In 2013, UNESCO listed this diet as part of the cultural heritage of countries around the Mediterranean, such as Greece, Italy, Spain, Morocco, Portugal, Croatia, and Cyprus.

In the beginning, I want to point out that by starting this diet, you will not magically and suddenly transform into a slender person without cholesterol issues.

Nothing happens overnight, but if you follow it regularly, this diet could help you lower the risk of heart and blood vessel illnesses by about 25%.

People who live in Mediterranean countries are known to be healthy, slender, and live longer. We cannot say the same for people who live fast-paced lives, eat junk and fast food, do not work out, and are exposed to stress every single day.

Don't get me wrong – people from the Mediterranean countries are not immune to diseases like heart attacks or cancer, but the risk of getting these illnesses is significantly lower.

The first thing you think about the Mediterranean is an amazing nature, great food, delicious wine, sunny days, and people who are friendly and content with their lives.

What is the secret for Mediterranean people being healthier and slender?

The answer is simple - they eat plenty of fresh and whole food. Fruits and vegetables are always on their menu. You would agree that some of the most delicious Mediterranean meals are so simple and have nothing else but vegetables and olive oil. Eating a diet based on fruits, vegetables, fish, nuts, and healthy oils, would make your body detox from all the artificial ingredients you stocked while eating junk and fast food. Providing your body with healthy nutrients, vitamins, minerals, proteins, healthy fats, and a reasonable amount in carbohydrates would lead to an easy slimming. Also, you would reduce the risk of getting diabetes, cholesterol, heart failures, and cancer.

The Mediterranean Diet is focused on whole-grain foods, healthy fats (olive oil, nuts, fish), fruits, vegetables, and small amounts of red meat (consumed rarely). So, how does it work?

The crucial thing about this diet is that it encourages you to cook your food, pay attention to it, dine with your family, and actually slow down when you consume your meal. This way, you pay attention to the flavors and how your food is cooked.

Of course, you can do this with any diet, but this diet has no processed food at all. Nothing contains added sugars or other ingredients to keep the food fresher for a longer time.

Your meals contain fresh and whole fruits and vegetables (picked from the tree and ground and delivered to your table). Also, you would consume lean meats like fish, olive oil, whole grains, and legumes and almost no processed food and sweets.

Providing your body with such quality ingredients would help it get what it needs, without making reserves of fats that will not be used. When consuming unhealthy foods rich in fats and carbs, your body uses the energy from the carbs, and the fats are stored (which is why there are layers of fat around your stomach, arms, and legs).

With a clean and healthy diet, your body gets to use the healthy ingredients, and to burn the fats (since there are no high amounts of carbs in your diet, your body seeks the second best energy source, which is the fat).

If you decide to start exercising, your diet will show even better results.

The most important thing, I believe you would love, is that this diet is not encouraging you to starve or skip meals. Every meal is important, and every meal must contain healthy ingredients.

You would start your day with a light breakfast. Sure, the light meal will not keep you full for a long time, so instead of going for a snack, you should get a piece of fruit such as berries, a banana, pear, or whatever fruit you like.

Your lunch is the next meal that includes plenty of vegetables combined with healthy fats such as olive oil, cheese, and nuts, and you would finish your day with a dish that contains fish and vegetables, and a glass of red wine.

Following this diet will not stop you from eating foods that have carbohydrates. In this diet, carbs are welcomed. After all, those delicious pasta dishes combined with cooked sauce are people's favorite.

Carbohydrates are not your enemy if they are consumed in the right amount and combined with healthy fats (seafood, fish, olive oil), and vegetables.They are only bad for your weight if it is the only thing you are eating and in large amounts without providing your body with healthy fats, proteins, vitamins, and minerals.

As I mentioned, a large amount of carbs helps the body focus on burning the carbs only so it can crate glucose which is the brains' main energy source.

The good thing about this diet is that it is so abundant, you can pick any recipe you want from French, Italian, Spanish, or Greek cuisine.

Also, you have already noticed I used the phrase eating pattern instead of a diet. It is because you are not restraining yourself from anything but high amounts of processed and junk food, and you get to eat clean, delicious, and healthy foods. It is more a pattern, which gives you the right to pick what foods you would eat and how many calories you would consume daily.

There is the so-called Mediterranean diet pyramid that would help you learn how to start and create your initial meal plan.

This pyramid's main focus is daily eating of vegetables, fruits, whole grains, nuts, olive oil, fish, seafood, beans, and legumes. These foods should be present in your menu at least five times a week.

Eggs, cheese, poultry, and yogurt should be consumed in lesser amounts, while sweets, soda drinks, heavy liquor, and red meat should be consumed rarely.

So, nothing is forbidden; there are only foods that should be your main go-to ingredients and foods that should be eaten only occasionally.

Perhaps you do not want to give up on alcohol, but this eating pattern allows red wine (in moderate amounts). One glass of red wine for women and two for men; if you are not a fan of wine, it is not a mandatory drink, of course.

So, if you are about to try this eating pattern because you want results overnight, I would have to break it down to you and disappoint you. You will have to be patient before you see results. The best way to slim down is to do it gradually over weeks and even months.One thing I can say for sure is that people tend to overeat when they are bored or alone when they have fast food within the reach in their desk or at home.

People constantly feel hunger even after eating a huge amount of calories. That is because you are only satisfying your flavor buds and not providing your body with what it needs. Junk food is packed in flavors that feel good and make you feel content. But, the results, in the long run, are not only obesity but health issues as well.So, what are the foods you should put on your list before starting this diet? Let's check in the following chapter.

HOW CAN YOU START?

The main question people have about this diet is how to start.

The truth is there is no special preparation when it comes to switching your diet from regular to the Mediterranean.

Start with clear goals of what you want to achieve. How much weight do you want to lose? How many calories per meal do you want to consume?

Let's say you are not content with your current weight, and you set a goal to lose ten pounds (4.5 kilograms). Now make a mental check of all the things you have been eating in the past few days. Or in general, think of the foods you are usually eating.

In most cases, people don't pay attention to the meals they are eating. Sure, fast food tastes great and gives you the feeling of fullness at least for a while. The truth about it is that it contains ingredients that are not good for your health, but you already know that. Fast food, junk food, and processed foods and drinks contain ingredients that will only satisfy your hunger immediately but will make you crave more in a little while.

And this is how you enter the wicked circle; the more you eat junk or processed food, the more you crave it.

If you had such habits, and now you want to start consuming healthy meals that will help you burn the fat, you can begin by emptying your fridge from all the processed and junk food that does not benefit your health.

Start by buying fresh fruits and vegetables. Prepare a bowl of soup or a salad and eat it with your lunch. Instead of indulging in chips or cookies, get a handful of nuts or a piece of fruit.

Start cooking with olive oil instead of butter, and forget about your favorite cans of soda. Instead of it, get a freshly squeezed juice and drink it in the morning.

Olive oil is the primary cooking oil in the Mediterranean diet. This diet does not exclude fat, but what is crucial is how healthy it is. Unlikely most diets that are reducing the use of fats, the Mediterranean diet is focused on the good fats (olives, avocado, olive oil).

16

Poly and monosaturated fats are good for your health. Keep the saturated and trans fats in low amounts (processed meats, French fries, fried onions, donuts, chips, cupcakes, junk food).

Fruits and vegetables should become the dominant foods in your meals.

You don't have to live in any Mediterranean country to provide your kitchen with foods that will help you cook such meals. It is enough to change your focus to a fresh and whole-grain food.

The most important thing to remember is that this is not a strict meal plan. It is just your choice of meals prepared with lots of vegetables, olive oil, legumes, beans, fish, and whole grains.

The sweets are not excluded but should not be consumed as frequently as the fruits.

If you eat meat and wonder how you will survive without it, there is no need to worry. Your main protein supplies will come from fish, but remember that beans, leafy greens, legumes, nuts, and dairy products also contain proteins in fewer amounts.

Again, meat-eaters must not worry about how they will start this diet when it recommends mostly fish because red meat and poultry are not excluded from it. Meat is present in this diet, but it is not recommended to be consumed as frequently as fish.

Eggs and fermented dairy products are also present in this diet, only in moderate amounts.

Once you switch to this way of eating, you will notice that you are no longer bloated, nor do you feel hungry. Every meal contains enough nutrients to keep you full, but healthy and light at the same time.

The Mediterranean Diet will help you regulate your cholesterol and will purify your blood; people with high blood pressure will have significant benefits.

How can you know if a food is right for you? Beginners need to focus on fresh foods, mainly. Mediterranean meals don't have recipes that will encourage you to use processed food. However, if you need to get processed food, check the ingredients; the fewer ingredients, it contains, the better it is.

Anything with more than three ingredients is not a good choice; all those additives are not doing your body any good. They were added to keep the product's shelf life longer.

Whole and fresh foods are the right choices, so you can never make a mistake by including them in your meals.

It may sound like a massive challenge for people who are used to eating meals that barely contain vegetables, let alone fruits in between meals.

A Mediterranean meal must contain an abundant amount of fresh vegetables and fruits.

This means that seven to ten servings of vegetables and fruits should be consumed every day. If this seems like a tremendous amount to you, you can begin with three to five vegetable and fruit servings per day. Even this amount is good enough to reduce the risk of cardiovascular problems.

Beginners, who are not used to such foods, can start the simplest way possible. For instance, anytime you prepare your eggs for breakfast, add some spinach or kale. Or you can add some avocado, tomatoes or cucumber to your sandwich; substitute your chocolate bars with an apple, a banana or a peach.

Every time you want to have red meat for lunch or dinner, go for a fish instead.

Mackerel, tuna, or salmon will provide you with enough proteins and omega-3 fatty acids. Shellfish are another excellent option; they are packed in lean proteins but don't contain that many omega-3 fatty acids.

Red meat or any other processed meats should be eaten less frequently.

When it comes to dairy products such as cheese, you are allowed to eat it. Instead, to eat processed cheese with a burger chose strong-flavored cheeses such as feta (in smaller amounts); processed cheese is not the best option (Cheddar, American).

As mentioned above, whole grains are an excellent choice in this diet. This is, as the name suggests, whole food; it comes in its original form, and it was not anyhow processed. You can add quinoa in your menu; start the day with well-cooked quinoa combined with some honey or cheese with intense flavor. Quinoa is an excellent "filler" for salads.

Barley is another great choice for beginners; it makes the perfect combination with any salad or main dish.

Oatmeal will help you go through your first Mediterranean diet breakfasts.

Popcorn is not excluded, but make sure you use olive oil for popping it (no butter in your popcorn; use some olive oil and salt instead).

DO I HAVE THE RIGHT INGREDIENTS TO START THIS DIET?

Now that you decided to start this eating pattern, you would have to get the ingredients.

There is no big philosophy here. You are allowed to get your favorite fruits, vegetables, seeds, nuts, and anything that grows in the garden.

This is not a vegan or vegetarian diet since you are allowed to eat fish and seafood, and occasionally red meat.

Fish and seafood should be on your table a few times a week.

When it comes to dairy food, it should be consumed in moderation, just like red meat.

Red wine is the drink you can always go to if you feel like having some alcohol. However, you should not drink it too often or in large amounts. A glass of red wine with your meal is more than enough.

Keep in mind that your food should be fresh (at least twice a day you should eat fruits and vegetables).

Also, if you want to follow the proper Mediterranean diet, you would have to start taking your meals seriously. This means, your meals should be cooked and enjoyed in peace without rushing.

Resting after a meal is very important. Most people cannot afford to rest after a meal, but if you have the chance to slow down a little bit and let your stomach digest your meal, do it without hesitation.

I would like to point out that this is not a harsh diet that will make you feel hungry; you will always have delicious meals on your menu. So, even if you decide to change your eating habits drastically, you will feel that something is missing on your plate.

What people love about it is that they do not have to accommodate to new foods. We have all tried tomatoes, fish, apples, watermelons, onions, garlic, olive oil.

Your body would not be stressed out by any new flavors. Your only challenge would be to adapt to a healthier lifestyle and end the habit of consuming sugary and processed foods. Allow yourself to take the time and transit to your menu slowly.

Here Are The Foods You Can Eat In This Diet.

I am sure you already have a bottle of *extra-virgin olive* oil at home. If not, now is the time to get one. Sure, you can cook with butter and any other oil, but it will mess up your diet and would not provide you with the healthy fats you need. Extra-virgin olive oil is great for fresh salads, cooking fish and seafood.

Provide your kitchen with *nuts and seeds*. Your regular processed snacks are not welcome in this diet. Instead, you would go for a healthy substitute. Start with pumpkin seeds, hazelnuts, walnuts, chia seeds, chickpeas, corn, or cashews.

You can combine them in your breakfasts, snacks, desserts, and even your dinner. They are rich in iron and proteins and will suppress your hunger in between meals.

Next, you should get *fish and seafood*. Some people are not fans of seafood; you can always start slowly. Red meat is not your friend. It is responsible for high cholesterol and triglycerides. Meat is not adding to your weight if eaten moderately. If consumed every day with a large number of carbohydrates like French fries and white bread, it would add weight and put your health at risk.

Your body needs the omega-3 fatty acids that are healthy and help you slim easily. Fish and seafood are the best foods for your health.

Known for its properties when it comes to improving your sight, strengthening your hair and nails, and lower the risk of heart failures, seafood and fish should be consumed at least twice a week. Omega-3 fatty acids work as an anti-inflammatory agent and are an excellent nutrient that helps in boosting your immunity but also in fighting depression and anxiety.

Of course, you cannot begin this diet without *fruits and veggies*. Onions, garlic, cucumber, peas, potatoes, zucchini, green beans, mushrooms, broccoli, you name it. Also, leafy greens like spinach, kale, lettuce should be on your menu. They are great for salads, pasta, and side dish. When it comes to fruit, go for your favorites; you cannot make a mistake with seasonal fruits like apples, bananas, or berries. Fruits are wonderful as snacks, but also as breakfast ingredients (combine them occasionally with Greek yogurt and oatmeal).

Beans and legumes should be on the table of every beginner. You would need lentils, beans, and chickpeas. These foods are great for your salads, but also as a side dish with your lunch or dinner.

I mentioned that *dairy products* are not recommended for everyday use, but you can still use them. Add some feta cheese, ricotta, Mozzarella, or parmesan in your breakfast, salads, or pasta.

Now, as mentioned above, this is not a diet that recommends frequent use of meat. But also, it is not a vegetarian or vegan diet, so the meat is not entirely excluded. If you do not want to give up on meat abruptly, include it once or twice a week, but in moderate amounts. *Beef and chicken* are great options.

When it comes to carbohydrates, *bread and pasta* are your friends. Sandwiches, pasta (spaghetti, macaroni, you name it) are not excluded. Just always make sure you consume bread and pasta made of whole grains.

Eggs are not excluded from this diet, so you do not have to quit them.

Although processed foods are not the best option (due to the heavy amount of added salt and sugars), *pantry food* is absolutely all right. You can use canned beans, tomatoes, corn, and chickpeas. To be sure you are consuming healthy ingredients, always read the ingredient list. Foods that have a long ingredient list are not your ideal option.

And finally, *herbs*; Mediterranean cuisines are so amazing and smell so inviting because of the herbs. Fresh cilantro, rosemary, black pepper, parsley, cumin, basil, dill, garlic, and onion should find a place in your kitchen. Of course, herbs are not mandatory, if you do not enjoy them.

The main ingredients to start the Mediterranean diet are seasonal veggies and fruits of your choice, nuts, bread, and pasta made of whole grain and fish and seafood.

HOW EASY IS TO FOLLOW THE MEDITERRANEAN DIET?

There is no right answer to this question. I can say it is easy for me, but for another person, it may not be the best option.

Here is why.

Some people spent their entire life eating foods like hamburgers, chips, soda drinks, processed foods and meats, and junk food. Their taste buds are used on those flavors. People who eat such foods are not necessarily unhealthy or overweight, but extended eating of such foods would take its toll in the later years of age.

Now, when a person whose diet is mainly focused on processed food tries to change it and begins to eat fresh and whole-food, they might not get used to it immediately.

Some people are not fans of fruits and vegetables and prefer eating their meat more frequently. Seafood and fish might not be everyone's favorite as well.

So it is not the food that is a problem but re-creating your old habits.

However, the good news is that transitioning into this way of eating is not a stress for your organism. Sure, you might have cravings for sweets and junk snacks, but that is normal. The body would want to have what it was used on.

So, in the beginning, you might feel like breaking your eating pattern with a giant hamburger with fries and a soda drink. But, once you allow yourself to adapt to the new meals, you would be surprised that you no longer crave anything.

The good thing about this diet is that it is not going to make you starve or eat super small dishes with foods you don't like.

From the food list in the previous chapter, you already saw that Mediterranean meals contain foods you already eat. There are no restrictions, only foods that are a priority and are consumed every day, and foods that should be consumed moderately.

Some people cannot imagine their day without a dairy product or eggs. The key lies in a slow transit. Reduce the foods you usually ate to twice or three times a week.

Don't let your brain think that something is forbidden (if you were ever on a diet, you know that the cravings are unbearable when foods are forbidden to you).

Every meal contains enough calories to keep you full, and you are allowed to eat healthy snacks (nuts, fruits, and veggies).

This is an eating pattern, and that is all you have to think of. You can combine your ingredients without counting calories. You will never be hungry, and by the end of your first week, you would be entirely used on your new meals.

Don't feel bad if you allow yourself to still eat the foods you used to eat before this diet. In fact, the best way to adapt to this diet is to start slowly.

Start with a few meals first. Instead of having your usual meat dish, substitute it with fish or seafood. See how your body reacts and if you like the taste.

Some people may find that Mediterranean meals are abundant in vegetables. Even if you love vegetables, this transition might be hard work for you. You might feel as if though you are hungry and that the vegetable stew did not satisfy your hunger.

Instead to jump for an entire vegetable meal, add a bowl of salad with your lunch or steam veggies with your chicken steak dinner.

The same goes for fruit. If you were used to eating fruit a few times a week in the past, it may be a challenge to eat two or three pieces of fruit on a daily basis. Create a habit to eat a piece of fruit every day with your breakfast or as a snack between your breakfast and lunch.

Another challenge could be to follow the diet if you tend to eat out more frequently (some people spend most of their day at work or school). You can always pick a Mediterranean meal, but when you are exposed to so many choices, you might 'fail' and go back to the foods you are now trying to avoid. This leads us to the fact that now you will have to start cooking your meals. This might be a huge challenge for some people. Some people simply hate cooking, they do not have the time for it or are not very skilled cooks.

No matter the fact that Mediterranean dishes do not require some extraordinary cooking skills, this could be a major setback for many people. If you want to still follow this diet and spend less time in the kitchen, you could cook a few meals in advance. Create your meal plan, cook, and store everything in glass containers in the freeze. Not only will you save time, but also electricity and energy.

Your first week is your best test. You would either dedicate yourself to it and see if you could last for a longer time, or you would simply give up and continue eating like before.

The most important thing is your willingness to make it. If you convince yourself that you would change your old unhealthy eating habits and you would endure it, there is no reason for you to fail.

Every transition is slow and even challenging. This is why you should test the waters first instead to dive in. Allow yourself to get familiar with the new tastes. Let your body adjust to the new nutrients.

This is a basic eating pattern for healthy eating. If your main goal is to lose weight without starving, the Mediterranean diet is your ideal first step.

None of the ingredients is strange to you (you surly have tasted fruits and vegetables and fish before). The unhealthy foods would still be on the menu, while you are progressing towards your new ways of eating.

There is everything in this diet, from proteins to fats, bread, pasta, fruits, veggies, nuts, and even wine.

At the end of the day, you will not feel different (as it could be the case with low carb, high in fat diets).

MEDITERRANEAN DIET HEALTH BENEFITS

This diet is known as perhaps the only one that provides you with good health in the long run. You will never feel hungry, nor will you feel as if though you are preventing yourself from eating delicious foods.

The only thing this diet requires is to reduce the consummation of unhealthy foods such as red meat, junk food, processed food, and sugars.

Mediterranean diet puts an accent on vegetables, fruits, seeds, fish, and legumes. You do not need to be a nutritionist or a doctor to know that a diet rich in such foods is a sure way to provide your body with healthy nutrients.

This diet is an extremely popular option for weight loss, but even if you are not willing to slim, you can switch to this diet because of the many health benefits it provides.People who have heart and cardiovascular issues, skin problems, diabetes, or simply want to stay healthy and lower the risk of evil diseases (like cancer), are advised to start the Mediterranean diet.

Let's take a look at the health benefits that this diet brings.

Reduced Risk of Heart Failures

Providing your body with colorful meals that contain large amounts of fruits, vegetables, healthy oils, and lesser processed food or unhealthy ingredients is a sure way to remain in good health.

New England Journal of Medicine published a study in 2013 that was following more than 7000 people (men and women) in Spain who were suffering type 2 diabetes. They were at high risk for cardiovascular illnesses; the ones that were following the Mediterranean diet (plenty of vegetables, fruits, fish, and olive oil) had about 30% lower risk of heart failures. The researchers did not encourage the participants to exercise (the study wanted to see only the results of the diet).

The study reanalyzed the data in 2018, and they came with similar results.

Consuming large amounts of fish instead of red meat is the key to a healthy heart; the risk for seizures, heart attacks, cholesterol, and early death is reduced.

32

Prevents Alzheimer's Disease and Memory Decline

The Mediterranean way of eating will help your brain stay in good shape. As we get older, our memory tends to decline, and the brain's activity significantly drops.

The human brain needs food in order to function properly, and when that food is not suitable, the risk of diseases such as Alzheimer's grows higher.

Our brains need quality nutrients and oxygen, and the best way to provide that is by the right foods.

Food that is not providing our blood with enough oxygen will manifest in poor memory and cognitive functioning.

In 2016 the Journal Frontiers in Nutrition was monitoring the effect of the Mediterranean diet on the cognitive functions. The results showed that this diet does improve brain functioning and slows down memory declining.

Weight Loss and Healthy Weight Maintenance

Switching from a regular (mostly unhealthy) diet to the Mediterranean pattern of eating is a very common thing. As mentioned in the previous chapters, this way of eating is not a new thing, nor was it created by nutritionists.

This is a regular lifestyle of the people who live around the Mediterranean (Spain, France, Italy, Balkan countries).

The menu consists of foods that are native to the area, especially fruits, vegetables, seeds, fish, nuts, herbs.

What makes this eating pattern so suitable for weight loss is the fact that it suggests consuming fresh and whole-food without additional additives that only add flavor and make you crave more unhealthy foods. The purging effect of fruits, vegetables, nuts, and healthy fats like olive oils cleanses your body from fat and cholesterol and helps in the slimming process.

The body is now provided with healthy nutrients that are easy for digestion. The healthy fats (olive oil, avocado, nuts) provide the brain and the body with sufficient amounts of energy, while the rest of the ingredients are not layered in fats all over the body.

Consuming this calorie-unrestricted Mediterranean eating pattern for five years will keep your weight balanced. The food combination in its suggested amounts (daily, weekly, and monthly) will result in a healthy weight loss.

If your goal is to lose a larger amount of weight, you can combine the Mediterranean diet with calorie restriction and physical activity.

Mediterranean Diet Helps in Managing Type 2 Diabetes

People who have type 2 diabetes are advised to follow diets that are not rich in carbohydrates and sugars. The Mediterranean diet might be a good solution for them, as well.

This diet is all about whole grains and healthy carbohydrates, which will not increase the blood sugar levels. Complex whole-grain carbohydrates (quinoa, wheat berries, or buckwheat) are a far better option than refined carbohydrates (white bread, sweets, juices, chocolate, fast food).

Studies show that people aged 50 to 80 years, who were diabetes-free and followed the Mediterranean diet for three to four years, did not develop the disease.

These people used olive oil and nuts, and in general, ate whole food and fish instead of processed food and meats. They had a 52% lower risk for type 2 diabetes.

Mediterranean Diet Reduces the Risk of Some Cancers

Food can be both cure and poison. When your daily menu contains foods rich in unhealthy fats (palm oil, butter), red meat, processed food, sugars, and large amounts of proteins (mostly from red meat) and carbohydrates (unhealthy options such as cookies, white bread, rice, French fries, etc.) – your body will suffer on the long run.

Most cancers are a result of poor eating habits, lack of physical activity, polluted air, and so on.

The Mediterranean diet helps in reducing the risk of cancers like colorectal, gastric, and breast cancer. The high intake of vegetables, fruits, and whole grains play a powerful role in keeping you healthy and in good shape.

Women who follow this diet (and use extra-virgin olive oil) have a 62% lower risk of breast cancer, studies show.

Mediterranean Diet Can Help With Anxiety and Depression

Almost everyone has experienced occasional depression (due to stress, problems in the family, or work).

Depression is a persistent loss of enthusiasm and enjoyment in doing things you once liked doing. Despair, lethargy, disinterest, sleeping problems are just a few of the symptoms of depression.

Anxiety, on the other hand, often manifests with nervousness before significant events, speaking to people, and meeting new people, going out, making mistakes, fear of arguments. Sweaty palms, irritable bowel movement, overthinking, lack of sleep, and intrusive thoughts that you are not good enough or not doing things good enough are just a few of the symptoms.

Psychologists say that diet and mental health are tightly connected. Foods packed in healthy ingredients can seriously improve your general health, including your energy levels and mental state.

If you are avoiding processed foods rich in unhealthy fats, red meat, white bread, and sugars, you will witness significant changes in every aspect of your life.

Change of the lifestyle (new eating habits and physical activity) can improve the depression and anxiety symptoms.

Good, healthy, and quality food impacts the mood and increases the levels of serotonin. When physical activity is added, depression becomes less severe. Naturally, you need to see professional help from a therapist, but a change of your diet could only bring positive shifts.

This diet also affects the immune system, which is one of the main factors in the risk of depression.

Mediterranean diet prevents inflammations, as well. Most bacteria are fed in sugars and processed food nutrients, so when you change that and provide your body with fresh food, fish, nuts, olive oil, and whole-grain carbohydrates, you are reducing the risk of inflammation.

When your body is at a high risk of inflammation, it is more prone to depression. According to the studies published in The Journal of Clinical Psychiatry, depressed people have a 46% higher risk of inflammatory diseases in their blood.

The Mediterranean diet is packed with anti-inflammatory foods – olive oil, leafy greens, nuts, salmon, sardines, oranges, strawberries are just some of the foods that fight inflammation. On the other hand, foods like margarine, red meat, processed meat, deep-fried foods, white bread, soft drinks (soda and tetra pack juices) are not recommended, not only because they are not healthy, but because they are known for their inflammatory properties.

HOW TO USE THE MEDITERRANEAN DIET FOR WEIGHT LOSS – MEAL PLAN

If you are one of the millions of people who were not satisfied with their weight at least once, you surely want to know how to use the Mediterranean diet for slimming healthily.

Now that we saw what ingredients and foods should take place in your kitchen, it is time to see how you can use them in your daily and weekly meals.

Most people who have started this way of eating remained true to it, because it has no strict rules. There are only general guidelines, and people apply them as they want.

Naturally, you need to stick to these general rules that require lesser use of red meats, unhealthy oils, dairy products, and sugars.

The beauty of the Mediterranean diet lies in the fact that it is up to you to figure out what foods are good for you.

For some people eating fish, every day seems like heaven, while others don't find it that good. While some love salmon and eat it three times a week, others may find shellfish a better option and consume it once or twice per week.

This is a diet that you can easily adapt to your lifestyle, and what is amazing is the fact that even if you often travel or have to go to a certain event (weddings, birthdays), you can still eat the proper foods without ruining your diet. Most people complain that they cannot follow their diet at work, while they travel or during the holidays. That won't be the case with this diet, which is why people tend to stick to it for such a long time.

The great thing about it is that you cannot get tired of the meals. Sure, we all love Italian cuisine, but once you feel like changing a meal but still keep it in the Mediterranean style, you can seek for recipes from the Spanish or French cuisine.

What I personally love about this diet is that you do not have to be the world's best chef to prepare a meal. We talk about using fresh ingredients such as tomatoes, potatoes, carrots, lettuce, apples, walnuts, bananas. And if we are speaking honestly, everyone can make one simple meal with most of these foods.

When it comes to breakfasts, a sandwich with an avocado and feta cheese will be a great option, and you don't have to know how to cook to make it.

Even if you are not the most skilled cook, you can always go for simpler recipes; everybody knows how to cook pasta and tomato sauce (fresh or from a can). There are millions fast and simple recipes for this diet, so there is no way you will get frustrated while cooking.

You will learn that fresh food comes before frozen or canned (processed food). Perhaps, that will be the biggest challenge. People's lifestyle these days is fast-paced, and none of us wants to spend a lot of time in the kitchen. But, since this is something you are doing for your own benefit, you will have to learn to enjoy picking the right foods, read the ingredients, and actually cook a little bit. The easiest way to start your first week is to prepare a meal plan. That requires buying the ingredients you know you will like to eat. If you are not a fan of strict plans, an abundance of fruits, vegetables, fish, olive oil, nuts, and legumes will help you go through it easier.

You can start your first day with a simple and light breakfast – Greek yogurt with some honey and your favorite berries.

To endure the time till lunch, get a handful of your favorite nuts. Lunch can be anything from a delicious tuna salad, lentils salad mixed with tomatoes and green or red peppers, seasoned with salt and pepper, and olive oil.

And finally, your dinner can be baked salmon with garlic or pasta (whole grain) with pesto or tomato sauce. Afternoon snacks can be anything from fruits, nuts, hummus with vegetables (carrots, for e.g.).

It is all up to you and your preferences.

All you need to do is create your menu (either strictly or roughly) and stick to it, without giving in to your cravings for sweets or junk processed snacks.

If the beginning seems overwhelming, set small goals; for instance if you manage to go through your first two meals, sticking to Mediterranean diet ingredients, reward yourself with dinner that contains a small amount of chicken, for example. Drink a glass of wine with your lunch or dinner.

This diet is not about torturing yourself, but getting used to a healthier lifestyle.

When it comes to weight loss, many people believe that the less they eat, the better results they will get. Remember, you are trying to slim down in a healthy way, not starve yourself and then return your lost weight in two days.

Set time of the day when you will have physical activity; walking, hiking, gym, Pilates, yoga, jogging, cycling, or gardening. It should not feel like an errand but a pleasure.

Finally, your mindset is crucial in anything that you do. If you start this new lifestyle with the belief that you are doing something nice for yourself, everything will go easily.

Forget about your scale; don't measure your weight every day, because it adds additional stress. Simply relax and become mindful about your food, how you spend your day, your thoughts, and the good time you have with your loved ones.

The Mediterranean diet is a balanced plant-based food, so your results are guaranteed. What is most important is that you enjoy it.

BREAKFAST RECIPES

BANANA STRAWBERRY OATS

 Cooking Difficulty: 1/10	Cooking Time: 15 minutes	Servings: 1

INGREDIENTS

- 1 tbsp. sliced almonds
- ½ c. oats
- ½ tsp. cinnamon
- 1 c. shredded zucchini
- ½ banana, mashed
- 1 c. water
- ½ c. sliced strawberries
- dash of sea salt
- 1 tbsp. flax meal
- ½ scoop of protein powder

STEP 1
First, combine oats, salt, water, and zucchini in a large saucepan.

STEP 2
Cook the mixture over medium-high heat and cook for 8 to 10 minutes or until the liquid is absorbed.

STEP 3
Now, spoon in all the remaining ingredients to the mixture and give everything a good stir.

STEP 4
Finally, transfer the mixture to a serving bowl and top it with almonds and berries. Serve and enjoy.

NUTRITIONAL INFORMATION
Calories: 386, Proteins: 23.7g, Carbs: 57.5g, Fat: 8.9g

PEACHES AND CREAM

 Cooking Difficulty: 2/10

 Cooking Time: 20 minutes

 Servings: 4

INGREDIENTS

- 1 tsp. cinnamon
- cooking spray
- 2 c. coconut cream
- 4 peaches, sliced

STEP 1

Grease a baking pan with the cooking spray and combine the peaches with the other ingredients inside.

STEP 2

Bake this at 360 degrees F for 20 minutes, divide into bowls and serve for breakfast.

NUTRITIONAL INFORMATION

Calories 338, Fat 29.2g, Carbs 21g, Protein 4.2g

CREAMY EGGS

 Cooking Difficulty: 3/10	Cooking Time: 15 minutes	Servings: 4

INGREDIENTS

- 8 whisked eggs
- 2 chopped spring onions
- 1 tbsp. olive oil
- ½ c. heavy cream
- salt
- black pepper
- ½ c. shredded mozzarella
- 1 tbsp. chopped chives

STEP 1

Ensure that you heat the pan, add the spring onions, toss and sauté them for 3 minutes.

STEP 2

Add the eggs mixed with the cream, salt, and pepper and stir into the pan.

STEP 3

Sprinkle the mozzarella, on top, cook the mix for 12 minutes, divide it between plates, sprinkle the chives on top, and serve.

NUTRITIONAL INFORMATION

Calories 220, Fat 18.5g, Carbs 1.8g, Protein 12.5g

55

BLUEBERRY & MINT PARFAITS

 Cooking Difficulty: 2/10	Cooking Time: 5 minutes	Servings: 4

NUTRITIONAL INFORMATION
Calories: 272, Fat: 8g, Protein: 10g, Carbs: 25g

INGREDIENTS

- 1½ c. wholegrain rolled oats
- 1 c. almond milk
- 2 c. Greek yogurt, unsweetened
- 1 c. fresh blueberries
- blackberries (optional)
- 4 freshly chopped mint leaves

STEP 1
Place the oats and almond milk into a bowl and stir together to combine (this helps the oats to soften).

STEP 2
Spoon the oat and almond milk mixture evenly into your 4 containers.

STEP 3
Place a drop of yogurt into each container on top of the oats (use half of the yogurt as you'll be adding another layer of it).

STEP 4
Divide half of the blueberries between the 4 containers and sprinkle on top of the yogurt.

STEP 5
Add another layer of yogurt and then another layer of blueberries (you can use them all up at this stage).

STEP 6
Sprinkle the fresh mint over the top of each parfait.

STEP 7
Cover and place into the fridge to store until needed!

CLASSIC APPLE OATS

 Cooking Difficulty: 3/10	Cooking Time: 15 minutes	Servings: 2

NUTRITIONAL INFORMATION
Calories: 232, Fat: 5.7 g, Carbs: 48.1 g, Protein: 5.2 g

INGREDIENTS

- ½ tsp. cinnamon
- ¼ tsp. ginger
- 2 apples make half-inch chunks
- ½ c. oats, steel cut
- 1½ c. water
- maple syrup
- ¼ tsp. salt
- clove
- ¼ tsp. nutmeg

STEP 1
Take Instant Pot and carefully arrange it over a clean, dry kitchen platform. Turn on the appliance.

STEP 2
In the cooking pot area, add the water, oats, cinnamon, ginger, clove, nutmeg, apple, and salt. Stir the ingredients gently.

STEP 3
Close the pot lid and seal the valve to avoid any leakage. Find and press the "Manual" cooking setting and set cooking time to 5 minutes.

STEP 4
Allow the recipe ingredients to cook for the set time, and after that, the timer reads "zero."

STEP 5
Press "Cancel" and press "NPR" setting for natural pressure release. It takes 8-10 times for all inside pressure to release.

STEP 6
Open the pot and arrange the cooked recipe in serving plates. Sweeten as needed with maple or agave syrup and serve immediately. Top with some chopped nuts, optional.

STRAWBERRY YOGURT

 Cooking Difficulty: 1/10	Cooking Time: 10 minutes	Servings: 4

INGREDIENTS

- 1 c. strawberry halved
- 4 c. greek yogurt
- ½ tsp. vanilla extract

STEP 1

In a bowl, combine the yogurt with the strawberry, and vanilla, toss and keep in the fridge for 10 minutes. Divide into bowls and serve f breakfast.

NUTRITIONAL INFORMATION
Calories: 79, Fat: 0.4 g, Carbs: 15 g, Protein: 1.3 g

AVOCADO SPREAD

 Cooking Difficulty: 1/10

 Cooking Time: 1 minutes

 Servings: 4

INGREDIENTS

- 2 peeled and pitted avocados, chopped
- 1 tbsp. olive oil
- 1 tbsp. minced shallots
- 1 tbsp. lime juice
- 1 tbsp. heavy coconut cream
- salt
- black pepper
- 1 tbsp. chopped chives

STEP 1

In a blender, combine the avocado flesh with the oil, shallots, and the other ingredients except for the chives.

STEP 2

Pulse well, divide into bowls, sprinkle the chives on top, and serve as a morning spread with whole grain bread.

NUTRITIONAL INFORMATION

Calories: 79, Fat: 0.4 g, Carbs: 15 g, Protein: 1.3 g

SALMON AND EGG MUFFINS

 Cooking Difficulty: 3/10	Cooking Time: 15 minutes	Servings: 6

NUTRITIONAL INFORMATION
Calories: 93, Fat: 6g, Protein: 8g, Carbs: 1g

INGREDIENTS

- 4 eggs
- 1/3 c. milk
- salt and pepper
- 1½ oz. smoked salmon, chopped
- 1 tbsp. chopped chives
- green onions, optional

STEP 1

Preheat the oven to 356 degrees Fahrenheit and grease 6 muffin tin holes with a small amount of olive oil.

STEP 2

Place the eggs, milk, and a pinch of salt and pepper into a small bowl and lightly beat to combine.

STEP 3

Divide the egg mixture between the 6 muffin holes, then divide the salmon between the muffins and place into each hole, gently pressing down to submerge in the egg mixture.

STEP 4

Sprinkle each muffin with chopped chives and place in the oven for about 8-10 minutes or until just set.

STEP 5

Leave to cool for about 5 minutes before turning out and storing in an airtight container in the fridge.

KIWI SPINACH SMOOTHIE

 Cooking Difficulty: 1/10	Cooking Time: 1 minutes	Servings: 1

INGREDIENTS

- 1 c. baby spinach
- 2 peeled kiwi, halved
- ½ c. apple juice
- 2 tbsps. flaxseed, ground
- ½ peeled banana
- 12 ice cubes

STEP 1

Using a blender, set in all your ingredients. Blend well until very smooth. Enjoy!

NUTRITIONAL INFORMATION

Calories: 284, Fat: 5.6 g, Carbs: 55.3 g, Protein: 5.9 g

RASPBERRIES BREAKFAST SCONES

 Cooking Difficulty: 3/10

 Cooking Time: 18 minutes

 Servings: 12

NUTRITIONAL INFORMATION
Calories: 133, Protein: 2g, Fat: 8g, Carbs: 4g

INGREDIENTS

- 3 beaten eggs
- 1½ c. almond flour
- ¾ c. fresh raspberries
- ½ c. stevia
- 2 tsps. pure vanilla extract
- 2 tsps. baking powder

STEP 1
Set the oven to 375 degrees F to preheat. Line a baking sheet with baking paper and set aside.

STEP 2
In a large mixing bowl, beat the eggs together with the stevia, vanilla extract, baking powder, and then almond flour.

STEP 3
Fold the raspberries into the batter until evenly combined.

STEP 4
Scoop the batter onto the prepared baking sheet, about 3 tablespoons per mound. Ensure there is at least 2 inches of space between each scone.

STEP 5
Bake the scones for 15 minutes, or until golden brown.

STEP 6
Transfer the scones to a cooling rack and allow to set for 10 minutes. Then, transfer to an airtight container and store in a cool, dry place for up to 3 days, or refrigerate for up to 5 days. Reheat before serving.

SAGE ZUCCHINI CAKES

Cooking Difficulty: 2/10	Cooking Time: 13 minutes	Servings: 4

INGREDIENTS

- 1 lb. grated zucchinis, drained
- salt
- black pepper
- 1 tbsp. almond flour
- 1 whisked egg
- 1 tbsp. chopped sage
- 2 tbsps. olive oil

STEP 1

In a bowl, combine the zucchinis with the flour and the other ingredients except for the oil, stir well and shape medium cakes out of this mix.

STEP 2

Ensure that you heat the pan, add the cakes, cook them for 5-6 minutes on each side, drain excess grease on paper towels, divide the cakes between plates and serve for breakfast.

NUTRITIONAL INFORMATION
Calories 320, Fat 13.32g, Carbs 10g, Protein 12.1g

CHIA PUDDING

Cooking Difficulty: 2/10	Cooking Time: 32 minutes	Servings: 2

INGREDIENTS

- 1/3 c. coconut cream
- 55 g chia seeds
- 2 tbsps. cacao
- 1 tbsp. swerve
- 1 tbsp. vanilla sugar
- 2 c. water
- 2 tbsps. herbal coffee

STEP 1

Brew the herbal coffee with some hot water until the liquid is reduced by half. Strain the coffee before mixing in with the vanilla, swerve, and coconut cream.

STEP 2

Add in the chia seeds and cacao nibs net. Pour into some cups and place in the fridge for 30 minutes before serving.

NUTRITIONAL INFORMATION

257 Calories, 20.25g Fats, 2.25g Net Carbs, 7gProtein

FABULOUS GINGER PANCAKES

 Cooking Difficulty: 3/10

 Cooking Time: 22 minutes

 Servings: 10

NUTRITIONAL INFORMATION

115.3 Calories, 0.8g Fats, 22.1g Net Carbs, and 5.7g Protein.

INGREDIENTS

- 1½ c. all-purpose flour
- 1 tsp. baking powder
- ¼ tsp. baking soda
- ¼ tsp. salt
- ½ tsp. ground ginger
- 1 tsp. ground cinnamon
- 1 egg
- ½ tsp. vanilla
- ¼ c. molasses
- 1½ c. water

STEP 1
Stir and mix the baking soda, salt, cinnamon, baking powder, all-purpose flour, and ginger in a bowl.

STEP 2
In a separate bowl, beat eggs and add molasses and vanilla. Continue beating until the mixture becomes smooth. Stir and mix in water until completely combined.

STEP 3
Combine the 2 above mentioned mixtures and stir.

STEP 4
Lubricate a griddle and heat over high heat.

STEP 5
Transfer the batter on the griddle. Cook until the edges are dry and the bubbles form.

STEP 6
Flip and continue the cooking process.

STEP 7
Repeat this process with the remaining batter.

KALO'S KALE-BEET SMOOTHIE

Cooking Difficulty: 1/10	Cooking Time: 1 minutes	Servings: 2

INGREDIENTS

- 1 c. kale, chopped
- 4 fl. oz. cranberry juice, unsweetened
- ¼ c. frozen blueberries
- ½ red beet
- 1 tbsp. flax seeds
- 1 tbsp. chia seeds
- 1 tbsp. milk thistle seed powder
- 1 tsp. green tea powder (matcha)
- water

STEP 1

In a high-speed blender, mix flax seeds, kale, milk thistle seed powder, green tea powder, beet, chia seeds, blueberries, and cranberry juice. Pour in water, enough to reach the fill line of the blender. Blend the mixture until smooth.

NUTRITIONAL INFORMATION

Calories: 120, Carbs: 19.5 g, Fat: 4 g, Protein: 3.3 g

TASTY OATMEAL MUFFINS

 Cooking Difficulty: 3/10

 Cooking Time: 30 minutes

 Servings: 2

INGREDIENTS

- ½ c. hot water
- ½ c. raisins
- ¼ c. ground flaxseed
- 2 c. rolled oats
- ¼ tsp. sea salt
- ½ c. walnuts
- ¼ tsp. baking soda
- 1 banana
- 2 tbsps. cinnamon
- ¼ c. maple syrup

STEP 1
Mix water with flaxseed and set aside for about 5 minutes.

STEP 2
Set the flaxsees mixture with the rest of the ingredients in a food processor. Blend well for approximately 30 seconds to get a semi-coarse batter.

STEP 3
Set the batter in cupcake liners and transfer in muffin tins.

STEP 4
Set oven to preheat at 350 degrees F and bake for 20 minutes.

STEP 5
Serve.

NUTRITIONAL INFORMATION
Calories: 133, Fat 2 g, Carbs 27 g, Protein 3 g

TOMATO AND EGGS SALAD

 Cooking Difficulty: 1/10

 Cooking Time: 3 minutes

 Servings: 4

INGREDIENTS

- 4 hard-boiled eggs, peeled and chopped
- 2 c. halved cherry tomatoes
- 1 c. pitted kalamata olives halved
- 1 c. arugula or spinach
- 2 chopped spring onions
- black pepper
- 1 tbsp. avocado oil

STEP 1

In a salad bowl, combine the tomatoes with the eggs and the other ingredients, toss, divide into smaller bowls and serve for breakfast.

NUTRITIONAL INFORMATION
Calories 126, Fat 8.6g, Carbs 6.9g, Protein 6.9g

SHRIMP AND EGGS MIX

 Cooking Difficulty: 3/10

 Cooking Time: 13 minutes

 Servings: 4

INGREDIENTS

- 8 whisked eggs
- 1 tbsp. olive oil
- ½ lb. deveined shrimp, peeled and chopped
- ¼ c. chopped green onions
- 1 tsp. sweet paprika
- black pepper
- 1 tbsp. chopped cilantro

STEP 1

Ensure that you heat the pan; add the spring onions, toss and sauté for 2 minutes.

STEP 2

Add the shrimp, stir, then cook for 4 minutes more.

STEP 3

Add the eggs, paprika, salt, and pepper, toss, then cook for 5 minutes more.

STEP 4

Divide the mix between plates, sprinkle the cilantro on top, and serve for breakfast.

NUTRITIONAL INFORMATION
Calories 227, Fat 13.3g, Carbs 2.3g, Protein 24.2g

FISH & SEAFOOD

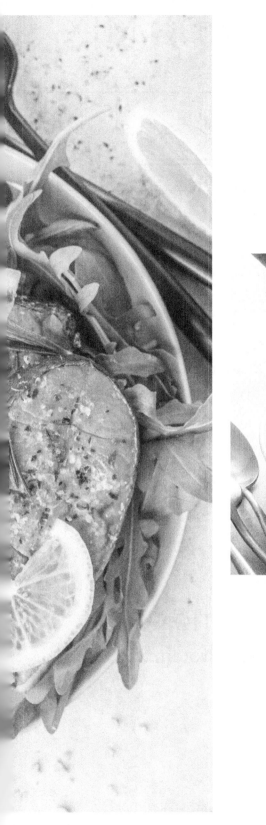

SHRIMP AND AVOCADO MIX

Cooking Difficulty: 2/10	Cooking Time: 8 minutes	Servings: 4

INGREDIENTS

- 1 lb. peeled shrimp, deveined
- 1 tbsp. avocado oil
- ½ c. chopped arugula
- salt
- black pepper
- 1 pitted avocado, peeled
- 2 tbsps. lime juice
- 2 tbsps. chopped parsley

STEP 1
Ensure that you heat the pan, add the shrimp then cook for 4 minutes.

STEP 2
Add the rest of the ingredients, cook over medium heat for 3 minutes more, divide into bowls, and serve.

NUTRITIONAL INFORMATION
Calories 240, Fat 12g, Carbs 5.6g, Protein 25g

SALMON AND TOMATOES

 Cooking Difficulty: 3/10	Cooking Time: 25 minutes	Servings: 4

INGREDIENTS

- 2 tbsps. avocado oil
- 4 boneless salmon fillets
- 1 c. halved cherry tomatoes
- 2 chopped spring onions
- ½ c. vegetable stock
- salt
- black pepper
- ½ tsp. dried rosemary

STEP 1

In a roasting pan, combine the fish with the oil and the other ingredients, introduce in the oven at 400 degrees F and bake for 25 minutes.

STEP 2

Divide between plates and serve.

NUTRITIONAL INFORMATION

Calories 200, Fat 12g, Carbs 3g, Protein 21g

LIME MACKEREL

 Cooking Difficulty: 3/10	Cooking Time: 25 minutes	Servings: 4

INGREDIENTS

- 4 boneless mackerel fillets
- 2 tbsps. lime juice
- 2 tbsps. olive oil
- salt
- black pepper
- ½ tsp. sweet paprika

STEP 1

Arrange the mackerel on a baking sheet lined with parchment paper, add the oil and the other ingredients, rub gently, introduce in the oven at 360 degrees F and bake for 30 minutes.

STEP 2

Divide the fish between plates and serve.

NUTRITIONAL INFORMATION

Calories 297, Fat 22.7g, Carbs 2g, Protein 21.1g

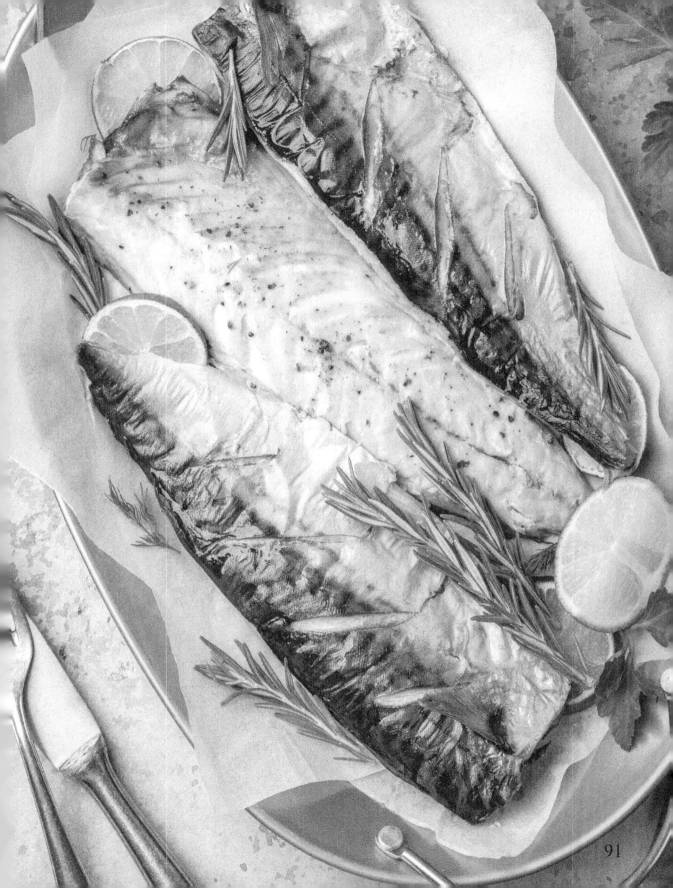

SALMON AND POTATO SALAD

Cooking Difficulty: 3/10	Cooking Time: 20 minutes	Servings: 6

INGREDIENTS

- 1 tbsp. chopped parsley
- 6 oz. salmon
- 1 chopped onion
- 1 tbsp. olive oil
- 3 baking potatoes
- basil leaves

STEP 1
Boil the potatoes until done. While those are boiling, heat up some oil in a pan and fry the onions.

STEP 2
Place the salmon slices into a dish and put the onions on top.

STEP 3
Top with the potatoes and sprinkle the parsley on top before serving and basil leaves.

NUTRITIONAL INFORMATION
120 Calories, 3.5g Fats, 20g Net Carbs, and 2g Protein

TASTY ROAST SALMON

 Cooking Difficulty: 3/10	Cooking Time: 23 minutes	Servings: 6

NUTRITIONAL INFORMATION
204.7 Calories, 10.4g Fats, 4.0g Net Carbs, 22.9g Protein

INGREDIENTS

- 1 medium size salmon
- 1 tbsp. olive oil
- 1 tbsp. white wine
- 1 tsp. paprika
- ½ tsp. ground ginger
- ½ tsp. crushed garlic
- 3 tsps. chopped parsley
- 1 lemon, cut into wedges

STEP 1

Preheat oven to 400F.

STEP 2

Line a roasting tin with foil, or alternatively simply coat the tin with a little bit of olive oil.

STEP 3

In a good size bowl mix together the garlic, ginger, paprika, chopped parsley and season with salt and pepper. Stir the mix well and then add in the salmon, gently rubbing the marinade over the fish.

STEP 4

Lay the salmon in the prepared tin and top it with a dash of white wine. Roast the fish uncovered for about 20 minutes.

STEP 5

Put the cooked tasty salmon in your serving dish decorated with your choice of herbs and lemon. Make sure pour the remaining juice over the fish.

WALNUT SALMON MIX

 Cooking Difficulty: 3/10

 Cooking Time: 10 minutes

 Servings: 4

INGREDIENTS

- 4 salmon fillets, boneless
- 2 tbsps. avocado oil
- salt
- black pepper
- 1 tbsp. lime juice
- 2 chopped shallots
- 2 tbsps. chopped nuts
- 2 tbsps. chopped parsley

STEP 1
Heat up a pan with the oil over medium-high heat; add the shallots, stir and sauté for 2 minutes.

STEP 2
Add the fish and the other ingredients, cook for 6 minutes on each side, divide between plates and serve.

NUTRITIONAL INFORMATION
Calories 276, Fat 14.2g, Carbs 2.7g, Protein 35.8g

ROASTED COD WITH BOK CHOY

Cooking Difficulty: 3/10	Cooking Time: 20 minutes	Servings: 4

NUTRITIONAL INFORMATION
355 Calories, 21g Fats, 3g Net Carbs, and 37g Protein

INGREDIENTS

- 24 oz. cod fillets
- ¾ lb. baby bok choy
- olive oil
- 1 tbsps. granulated garlic
- salt
- black pepper

STEP 1
Set the oven to 400 degrees F to preheat.

STEP 2
Cut out 3 sheets of aluminum foil, each large enough to completely cover one cod fillet.

STEP 3
Place a cod fillet on each sheet of aluminum foil then add the olive oil and granulated garlic. Add the bok choy, then season everything with salt and pepper.

STEP 4
Fold over the pouches and crimp the edges. Arrange on a baking sheet.

STEP 5
Bake for 20 minutes, then transfer to a cooling rack.

STEP 6
Let cool slightly, then refrigerate for up to 3 days. Reheat in the oven before serving.

CHIVES TROUT

 Cooking Difficulty: 3/10	Cooking Time: 7 minutes	Servings: 4

INGREDIENTS

- 4 boneless trout fillets
- 2 shallots, chopped
- salt
- black pepper
- 3 tbsps. chopped chives
- 2 tbsps. avocado oil
- 2 tsps. lime juice

STEP 1

Ensure that you heat the pan, add the shallots, and sauté them for 2 minutes.

STEP 2

Add the fish, and the rest of the ingredients cook for 5 minutes on each side, divide between plate and serve.

NUTRITIONAL INFORMATION

Calories 320, Fat 12g, Carbs 2g, Protein 24g

GINGER SESAME HALIBUT

 Cooking Difficulty: 3/10	Cooking Time: 17 minutes	Servings: 3

INGREDIENTS

- 24 oz. halibut fillets
- 1½ tbsps. minced fresh ginger
- 1½ tsps. soy sauce
- ½ tsps. worcestershire sauce
- 1½ tsps. olive oil
- ¾ tsp. sesame oil
- ¾ tsp. rice wine vinegar

STEP 1
Set the oven to 400 degrees F to preheat. Line a baking sheet with aluminum foil and set aside.

STEP 2
Combine the sesame and olive oils in a bowl, then stir in the rice vinegar, soy sauce, worcestershire sauce and ginger.

STEP 3
Add the fish fillets and turn several times to coat. Arrange the fish fillets on the prepared baking sheet. Bake for 17 minutes, or until done.

STEP 4
Cover each fish fillet with aluminum foil and refrigerate for up to 3 days, or freeze for up to 2 weeks. Reheat before serving.

NUTRITIONAL INFORMATION
237 Calories, 35g Fats, 1g Net Carbs, and 33g Protein

SHRIMP AND ZUCCHINI PAN

Cooking Difficulty: 2/10	Cooking Time: 8 minutes	Servings: 4

INGREDIENTS

- 1 tbsp. olive oil
- 1 lb. deveined shrimp, peeled
- 1 c. sliced zucchinis
- 2 chopped shallots
- 1 tbsp. granulated garlic
- 1 tbsp. red chili flakes
- salt
- 1 tbsp. chopped basil

STEP 1

Heat up a pan with the oil and ghee over medium heat; add the shallots and the garlic, stir and sauté for 2 minutes.

STEP 2

Add the shrimp, zucchinis, and the other ingredients, cook everything for 6 minutes more, divide between plates and serve for lunch.

NUTRITIONAL INFORMATION
Calories 176, Fat 5.5g, Carbs 4.2g, Protein 26.5g

SHRIMP ZOODLES

Cooking Difficulty: 2/10	Cooking Time: 6 minutes	Servings: 4

INGREDIENTS

- 1 lb. shrimp
- 4 c. zoodles
- 1 tbsp. chopped basil
- 1 c. vegetable stock
- 2 minced garlic cloves
- 2 tbsps. olive oil
- ½ tsp. paprika
- ½ lemon

STEP 1

Set your Instant Pot to SAUTÉ and melt the olive oil in it.

STEP 2

Add garlic and cook for 1 minute. Add the lemon juice and shrimp and cook for another minute.

STEP 3

Stir in the remaining ingredients and close the lid.

STEP 4

Set the Instant Pot to MANUAL and cook at low pressure for 5 minutes.

STEP 5

Do a quick pressure release. Serve and enjoy!

NUTRITIONAL INFORMATION

277 Calories, 15.6g Fat, 5.9g Carbs, 27.5g Protein

SALMON CUTLETS

Cooking Difficulty: 3/10	Cooking Time: 15 minutes	Servings: 3

INGREDIENTS

- 6 oz. salmon
- 1 small sweet potato
- 1 egg
- 1 tsp. pepper
- 1 tsp. salt
- 2 tbsps. fresh dill
- 2 tbsp. melted coconut oil
- 2 sliced scallions

NUTRITIONAL INFORMATION
260 Calories, 8g Carbs, 28g Protein, 12g Fat

STEP 1

Pre-heat your oven to 425 degrees Fahrenheit. Drain the canned salmon.

STEP 2

Microwave the sweet potato for 2 minutes or until tender and can be cut easily. Don't forget to poke holes in it before placing it in the microwave.

STEP 3

In a big bowl, combine the egg, pepper, salmon, scallions and dill.

STEP 4

Slice the sweet potato in half and remove the skin. Allow cooling. Add it into the salmon mix.

STEP 5

Use parchment paper to line a baking sheet, brush melted coconut oil on it.

STEP 6

Scoop 1/3 c. of salmon mixture and place it on the baking sheet. Flatten into half-inch thick, make sure that the thickness is even throughout.

STEP 7

Bake for 20 mins. then flip and cook until the patties start to brown for 10 minutes or cooked through.

STEP 8

Serve together with tartar sauce or with English muffins.

PAPRIKA SHRIMP MIX

 Cooking Difficulty: 3/10	Cooking Time: 10 minutes	Servings: 4

INGREDIENTS

- 1 lb. peeled shrimp, deveined
- 3 minced garlic cloves
- 2 minced shallots
- 2 tbsps. olive oil
- juice of 1 lime
- 2 tsps. sweet paprika
- 2 tbsps. chopped parsley

STEP 1
Ensure that you heat the pan, add the garlic and the shallots, stir, then cook for 2 minutes.

STEP 2
Add the shrimp and the other ingredients, cook over medium heat for 8 minutes more, divide between plates and serve.

NUTRITIONAL INFORMATION
Calories 205, Fat 9.1g, Carbs 4.1g, Protein 26.2g

SPICY HALIBUT IN CUMIN SPICE

Cooking Difficulty: 3/10	Cooking Time: 29 minutes	Servings: 2

NUTRITIONAL INFORMATION
Calories: 160, Fat: 4g, Carbs: 8g, Protein: 22g

INGREDIENTS

- 2 halibut steaks
- ¾ tsp. hot paprika
- 5 garlic cloves
- 1 tsp. dill weed
- 1½ tsp. ground cumin
- 1 tbsp. extra–virgin olive oil
- ½ tsp. black pepper
- 1 lime juice, freshly squeezed

STEP 1
Put together cumin, garlic, lime juice, hot paprika, dill and pepper In a food processor. Process for 1–2 minutes or until all the ingredients are combined well.

STEP 2
Rub processed mixture into the halibut steaks. Allow the mixture to meld and be absorbed by the fish for 25 minutes.

STEP 3
After 25 minutes, layer the fish steaks into the Instant Pot Pressure Cooker. Close the lid carefully. Press the "pressure" button and cook for 5 minutes.

STEP 4
When the timer beeps, choose the quick pressure release. This would take 1–2 minutes. Remove the lid.

STEP 5
Turn off the pressure cooker. Carefully remove the lid.

STEP 6
Remove fish and transfer to a platter. Serve with cumin spice mixture on the side.

GARLIC CALAMARI MIX

 Cooking Difficulty: 2/10	Cooking Time: 25 minutes	Servings: 4

INGREDIENTS

- 3 minced garlic cloves
- 2 tbsps. olive oil
- 1 lb. calamari rings
- 1 tbsps. balsamic vinegar
- 1 c. vegetable stock
- salt
- black pepper
- ¼ c. chopped parsley

STEP 1
Ensure that you heat the pan, add the garlic, stir, then cook for 5 minutes.

STEP 2
Add the calamari and the other ingredients toss bring to a simmer then cook over medium heat for 20 minutes.

STEP 3
Divide the mix into bowls and serve.

NUTRITIONAL INFORMATION
Calories 240, Fat 12g, Carbs 5.6g, Protein 25g

MEDITERRANEAN SHRIMP AND STRAWBERRY SALAD

Cooking Difficulty: 2/10	Cooking Time: 5 minutes	Servings: 4

INGREDIENTS

- 2 tbsps. balsamic vinegar
- 1 endive, shredded
- 2 c. strawberries halved
- 1 c. baby spinach
- 1 tbsp. lime juice
- 2 garlic cloves, minced
- 1 lb. shrimp, peeled and deveined
- 2 tbsps. olive oil
- feta cheese optional

STEP 1
Heat up a pan with the oil over medium-high heat, add the garlic and brown for 1 minute.

STEP 2
Add the shrimp and lime juice, toss and cook for 3 minutes on each side.

STEP 3
In a salad bowl, combine the shrimp with the endive, and the other ingredients, toss and serve for lunch.

NUTRITIONAL INFORMATION
Calories 260, Fat 9.7g, Carbs 16.5g, Protein 28g

SHRIMP SALAD

 Cooking Difficulty: 2/10	Cooking Time: 8 minutes	Servings: 4

INGREDIENTS

- 1 lb. shrimp, deveined and peeled
- 1 red onion, sliced
- ¼ tsp. black pepper
- 2 c. baby arugula
- 1 tbsp. lemon juice
- 1 tbsp. olive oil

STEP 1

Heat up a pan with the oil over medium heat, add the onion, stir and sauté for 2 minutes.

STEP 2

Add the shrimp and the other ingredients, toss, cook for 6 minutes, divide into bowls and serve for lunch.

NUTRITIONAL INFORMATION

Calories 341, Fat 11.5g, Carbs 17.3g, Protein 14.3g

SHRIMP AND MUSHROOM MIX

 Cooking Difficulty: 3/10

 Cooking Time: 15 minutes

 Servings: 4

INGREDIENTS

- ½ lb. sliced baby bell mushrooms
- 1 lb. peeled shrimp, deveined
- 2 tbsps. olive oil
- salt
- black pepper
- 1 tsp. crushed red pepper flakes
- 2 minced garlic cloves
- 1 c. heavy cream

STEP 1
Ensure that you heat the pan, add the garlic and the pepper flakes then cook for 2 minutes.

STEP 2
Add the mushrooms, toss, then cook for 5 minutes more.

STEP 3
Add the shrimp and the other ingredients, toss, cook over medium heat for 8 minutes more, divide into bowls and serve.

NUTRITIONAL INFORMATION
Calories 455, Fat 6g, Carbs 4g, Protein 13g

POULTRY RECIPES

CHICKEN AND MUSHROOMS

 Cooking Difficulty: 3/10

 Cooking Time: 15 minutes

 Servings: 4

INGREDIENTS

- ½ tsp. chili flakes
- 1 tbsp. olive oil
- black pepper
- ½ lb. white mushrooms halved
- 2 tbsps. olive oil
- 2 chicken breasts, skinless, deboned and halved

STEP 1
Heat up a pan with the oil over medium-high heat, add the mushrooms, toss and sauté for 5 minutes.

STEP 2
Add the meat, toss and cook for 5 minutes more.

STEP 3
Add the other ingredients, bring to a simmer and cook over medium heat for 5 minutes.

STEP 4
Divide the mix between plates and serve.

NUTRITIONAL INFORMATION
Calories 455, Fat 6g, Carbs 4g, Protein 13g

FIVE SPICE CHICKEN BREAST

 Cooking Difficulty: 3/10

 Cooking Time: 26 minutes

 Servings: 4

INGREDIENTS

- black pepper
- 1 tsp. five spice
- 1 tbsps. hot pepper
- 1 tbsp. avocado oil
- 1 tbsp. cilantro, chopped
- 2 chicken breast halves, skinless, deboned, and halved
- 1 c. tomatoes, crushed
- 2 tbsps. coconut aminos

STEP 1
Heat up a pan with the oil over medium heat, add the meat and brown it for 2 minutes on each side.

STEP 2
Add the tomatoes, five spice, and the other ingredients, bring to a simmer, and cook over medium heat for 30 minutes.

STEP 3
Divide the whole mix between plates and serve.

NUTRITIONAL INFORMATION
Calories 244, Fat 8.4g, Carbs 4.5g, Protein 31g

ROASTED CHICKEN SANDWICH WITH SPROUTS

Cooking Difficulty: 2/10	Cooking Time: 3 minutes	Servings: 1

INGREDIENTS

- 2 slices bread
- ¾ tbsp. mayonnaise
- ½ tsp. mustard
- ½ breast roasted chicken, thinly sliced
- 2 slices havarti or swiss cheese
- salt
- pepper
- sprouts or alfalfa
- ripe avocado
- tomato slices optional

STEP 1
Slice the chicken breasts and reheat in the microwave.

STEP 2
Spread bottom bread with mustard. Top with chicken and cheese. In a bowl, season the sprouts with salt and pepper. Spread the top bread with mayonnaise. Top with sprouts.

STEP 3
If want to reduce the mayonnaise, you can replace half the amount with pitted avocado. Or, you can simply add thin slices of avocados before you top the sprouts.

NUTRITIONAL INFORMATION
Calories: 195, Fat: 17g, Protein: 37g, Carbs: 24.62g

CHEESY TURKEY PAN

 Cooking Difficulty: 3/10	Cooking Time: 25 minutes	Servings: 4

INGREDIENTS

- 2 c. grated cheddar cheese
- 1 boneless turkey breast, skinless and cubed
- 1 tbsp. tomato passata
- ¼ c. veggie stock
- 1 tbsp. olive oil
- 2 chopped shallots
- ¼ c. cubed tomatoes
- salt and black pepper
- pasta

STEP 1
Ensure that you heat the pan; add the shallots and sauté for 2 minutes.

STEP 2
Add the meat and brown for 5 minutes.

STEP 3
Add the pasta and the other ingredients except for the cheese toss, then cook over medium heat for 10 minutes more.

STEP 4
Sprinkle the cheese on top, cook everything for 7-8 minutes, divide between plates, and serve for lunch.

NUTRITIONAL INFORMATION
Calories 309, Fat 23.1g, Carbs 3.9g, Protein 21.6g

CHICKEN CASSEROLE

 Cooking Difficulty: 3/10

 Cooking Time: 45 minutes

 Servings: 4

INGREDIENTS

- 1 lb. skinless chicken breast, boneless and ground
- 2 chopped shallots
- 1 tbsp. melted coconut oil
- 1 c. baby spinach
- 4 whisked eggs
- ½ c. grated parmesan
- salt and black pepper
- ½ tsp. garlic powder

STEP 1
Ensure that you heat the pan, add the shallots, stir, then cook for 5 minutes.

STEP 2
Add the meat and brown for 5 minutes more.

STEP 3
Add the eggs mixed with the garlic and toss.

STEP 4
Sprinkle the parmesan on top, introduce in the oven and bake at 390 degrees F for 35 minutes.

STEP 5
Divide the mix between plates and serve.

NUTRITIONAL INFORMATION
Calories 273, Fat 13.7g, Carbs 2.2g, Protein 34.5g

THYME CHICKEN MIX

 Cooking Difficulty: 3/10

 Cooking Time: 20 minutes

 Servings: 4

INGREDIENTS

- 1 lb. skinless and boneless chicken breast, sliced
- 1 tbsp. olive oil
- 2 chopped spring onions
- 1 c. baby spinach
- 1 tbsp. chopped thyme
- ½ c. tomato passata
- salt
- black pepper

STEP 1

Ensure that you heat the pan, add the spring onions, and the meat and brown for 5 minutes.

STEP 2

Add the rest of the ingredients, bring to a simmer then cook over medium heat for 15 minutes, stirring from time to time. Divide the mix into bowls and serve.

NUTRITIONAL INFORMATION
Calories 380, Fat 40g, Carbs 1g, Protein 17g

MEDITERRANEAN CHICKEN COUSCOUS

 Cooking Difficulty: 2/10	Cooking Time: 17 minutes	Servings: 8

INGREDIENTS

- 3 c. chopped chicken
- 1 ¼ c. chicken broth
- basil leaves
- 1 pint grape tomatoes
- 1 tsp. lemon rind
- 1 ½ tbsps. fresh lemon juice
- 1 5.6 oz. package of toasted pine nut couscous mix
- ¼ c. chopped fresh basil
- 1 4oz. package feta cheese
- ¼ tsp. pepper

STEP 1

You will want to begin this by heating the chicken broth and the seasoning packet from the couscous in a microwave for three to five minutes while on high.

STEP 2

Once the broth is boiling, mix it with the couscous in a large bowl and allow it to stand for about five minutes.

STEP 3

Once the time has passed, fluff the couscous with a fork and stir in the chicken.

STEP 4

When this is complete, mix in your spices and your meal is complete!

NUTRITIONAL INFORMATION

334 Calories, 10.9g Fat, 35.8g Carbs, 20.9g Protein

PESTO CHICKEN PASTA

Cooking Difficulty: 3/10	Cooking Time: 12 minutes	Servings: 6

INGREDIENTS

- 6 chicken breasts
- 2 c. gemelli pasta
- 8 oz pesto
- 28 oz. crushed tomatoes
- 1 c. water
- 2 c. baby spinach
- salt
- pepper
- grated parmesan cheese

STEP 1

Place the chicken, dry pasta, pesto, tomatoes, water, and baby spinach into the Instant Pot, stir to combine. Season with salt and pepper.

STEP 2

Close the lid and turn the sealing vent to "Sealing."

STEP 3

Select "Soup/Stew" or "Manually High Pressure" and set the cook time for 10 minutes.

STEP 4

Once completed, perform a "Quick Pressure Release" by opening the valve to "venting."

STEP 5

Plate the pasta and top with the grated Parmesan, if desired.

NUTRITIONAL INFORMATION

294 Calories, 18g Fat, 6.1g Carbs, 24.2g Protein

CHICKEN AND SPINACH SALAD

 Cooking Difficulty: 2/10

 Cooking Time: 3 minutes

 Servings: 4

INGREDIENTS

- ¼ tsp. black pepper
- 1 red onion, chopped
- 2 rotisserie chicken, de-boned, skinless and shredded
- ¼ c. walnuts, chopped
- 1 lb. cherry tomatoes, halved
- green pea
- 2 tbsps. lemon juice
- 1 tbsp. olive oil
- 4 c. baby spinach

STEP 1

In a salad bowl, combine the chicken with the tomato and the other ingredients, toss and serve for lunch.

NUTRITIONAL INFORMATION

Calories 380, Fat 40g, Carbs 1g, Protein 17g

VEGETABLES

BLACK BEAN STUFFED SWEET POTATOES

 Cooking Difficulty: 4/10	Cooking Time: 80 minutes	Servings: 4

NUTRITIONAL INFORMATION
Calories: 387, Fat: 16.1 g, Carbs: 53 g, Protein: 10.4 g

INGREDIENTS

- 4 sweet potatoes
- 15 oz. cooked black beans
- ½ tsp. ground black pepper
- ½ red onion, peeled, diced
- ½ tsp. sea salt
- ¼ tsp. onion powder
- ¼ tsp. garlic powder
- ¼ tsp. red chili powder
- ¼ tsp. cumin
- 1 tsp. lime juice
- 1 ½ tbsps. olive oil
- ½ c. cashew cream sauce

STEP 1
Spread sweet potatoes on a baking tray greased with oil and bake for 65 minutes at 350 degrees f until tender.

STEP 2
Meanwhile, prepare the sauce, and for this, whisk together the cream sauce, black pepper, and lime juice until combined, set aside until required.

STEP 3
When 10 minutes of the baking time of potatoes are left, heat a skillet pan with oil. Add in onion to cook until golden for 5 minutes.

STEP 4
Then stir in spice, cook for another 3 minutes, stir in bean until combined and cook for 5 minutes until hot.

STEP 5
Let roasted sweet potatoes cool for 10 minutes, then cut them open, mash the flesh and top with bean mixture, cilantro and avocado, and then drizzle with cream sauce.

STEP 6
Serve straight away.

VEGETARIAN RATATOUILLE

 Cooking Difficulty:
3/10

 Cooking Time:
40 minutes

 Servings:
4

INGREDIENTS

- 2 sliced red onions
- 1 sliced eggplant
- 2 sliced curettes
- 1 sliced red bell pepper
- 2 sliced squashes
- 2 c. tomato sauce
- ¼ c. parmesan cheese
- a handful of oregano & thyme

STEP 1
Set your oven to 375 F.

STEP 2
Stir the tomato sauce into a ceramic baking dish. Sprinkle the half of parmesan cheese over the sauce.

STEP 3
Pick one slice of each vegetable and line them up nicely. Arrange slices in baking dish and repeat the same order. Finish with a sprinkle of remaining parmesan cheese, and herbs.

STEP 4
Cook for 35-40 minutes until the vegetables are cooked through and a little crisp.

NUTRITIONAL INFORMATION
120 Calories, 3.5g Fats, 20g Net Carbs, and 2g Protein

BLACK BEAN AND QUINOA SALAD

Cooking Difficulty: 2/10	Cooking Time: 5 minutes	Servings: 10

INGREDIENTS

- 15 oz. cooked black beans
- 1 chopped red bell pepper, cored
- 1 c. quinoa, cooked
- 1 cored green bell pepper, chopped
- ½ c. vegan feta cheese, crumbled

STEP 1
In a bowl, set in all ingredients, except for cheese, and stir until incorporated.

STEP 2
Top the salad with cheese and serve straight away.

NUTRITIONAL INFORMATION
Calories: 64, Fat: 1 g, Carbs: 8 g, Protein: 3 g

BALSAMIC-GLAZED ROASTED CAULIFLOWER

Cooking Difficulty: 3/10	Cooking Time: 75 minutes	Servings: 4

NUTRITIONAL INFORMATION
Calories: 86, Fat: 5.7 g, Carbs: 7.7 g, Protein: 3.1 g

INGREDIENTS

* 1 head cauliflower
* ½ lb. green beans, trimmed
* 1 peeled red onion, wedged
* 2 c. cherry tomatoes
* ½ tsp. salt
* ¼ c. brown sugar
* 3 tbsps. olive oil
* 1 c. balsamic vinegar
* 2 tbsps. chopped parsley, for garnish

STEP 1

Place cauliflower florets in a baking dish, add tomatoes, green beans, and onion wedges around it, season with salt, and drizzle with oil.

STEP 2

Pour vinegar in a saucepan, stir in sugar, bring the mixture to a boil and simmer for 15 minutes until reduced by half.

STEP 3

Brush the sauce generously over cauliflower florets and then roast for 1 hour at 400 degrees f until cooked, brushing sauce frequently.

STEP 4

When done, garnish vegetables with parsley and then serve.

GARLICKY KALE & PEA SAUTÉ

 Cooking Difficulty: 2/10

 Cooking Time: 8 minutes

 Servings: 2

INGREDIENTS

- 2 sliced garlic cloves
- 1 chopped hot red chile
- 2 tbsps. olive oil
- 2 bunches chopped kale
- 1 lb. frozen peas

STEP 1

In a saucepot, mix the ingredients except peas. Cook until the kale becomes tender for about 6 minutes.

STEP 2

Add peas and cook for 2 more minutes.

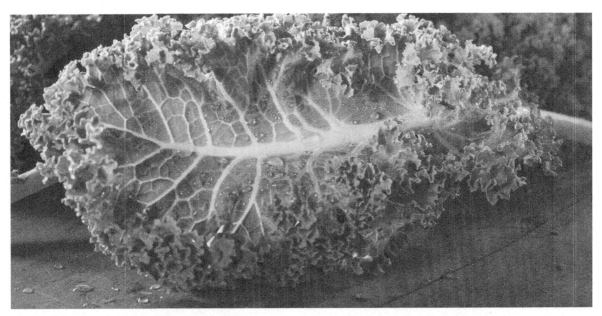

NUTRITIONAL INFORMATION

85 Calories, 3g Fats, 11g Net Carbs, and 5g Protein

SUN-DRIED TOMATO PESTO PASTA

 Cooking Difficulty: 2/10	Cooking Time: 11 minutes	Servings: 5

INGREDIENTS

- 1 c. fresh basil leaves
- 6 oz. sun-dried tomatoes
- 1 tbsp. lemon juice
- ½ tsp. salt
- ¼ c. olive oil
- ¼ c. almonds
- 3 minced garlic cloves
- ½ tsp. chopped red pepper flakes
- 8 oz. pasta

STEP 1
Cook the pasta according to the given instructions. For making, the pesto toasts the almonds over medium flame in a small skillet for around 4 minutes.

STEP 2
In a blender, put sun-dried tomatoes, basil, garlic, lemon juice, salt, red pepper flakes, and toasted almonds and blend it. While blending adds olive oil in it and blend it until it converts in the form of a pesto.

STEP 3
Now coat the pasta with the pesto and serve it.

NUTRITIONAL INFORMATION
Calories 256, Fat 13.7g, Carbs 28.1g, Protein 6.7g

CREAM CARROT SOUP

 Cooking Difficulty: 3/10	Cooking Time: 24 minutes	Servings: 4

INGREDIENTS

- ¼ tsp. black pepper
- 1 tbsp. cilantro, chopped
- 1 onion
- 1 tsp. turmeric powder
- 5 c. vegetable broth
- 1 lb. carrots, peeled and chopped
- 2 tbsps. olive oil
- 4 celery stalks, chopped

STEP 1

Heat up a pot with the oil over medium heat, add the onion, stir and sauté for 2 minutes.

STEP 2

Add the carrots and the other ingredients, bring to a simmer and cook over medium heat for 20 minutes.

STEP 3

Blend the soup using an immersion blender, ladle into bowls and serve.

NUTRITIONAL INFORMATION

Calories 221, Fat 9.6g, Carbs 16g, Protein 4.8g

LEMON ARUGULA SALAD

 Cooking Difficulty: 2/10	Cooking Time: 12 minutes	Servings: 5

NUTRITIONAL INFORMATION
164.3 Calories, 15.6g Fats, 5.7g Net Carbs, 3.5g Protein

INGREDIENTS

- 1 lemon
- ½ tsp. sugar
- 5 oz. arugula
- 2 tbsps. extra virgin olive oil
- 2 oz. shaved Parmesan cheese
- cashew nut

STEP 1

With a paring knife, cut top and bottom off the lemon. Cut peel and pith away from lemon; then, into a small bowl, cut segments from between membranes. Cut each segment in half. Squeeze 1 tbsp. juice from pulp. Sprinkle sugar over lemon segments; let stand at least 10 minutes.

STEP 2

In a large bowl, mix arugula with oil, lemon segments, juice, 1/4 tsp. salt and 1/2 tsp. coarsely ground black pepper.

STEP 3

Gently fold in Parmesan.

STEP 4

To serve, shave additional Parmesan on top if desired.

STEP 5

Serve immediately.

SPICE-ROASTED CARROTS

 Cooking Difficulty: 3/10	Cooking Time: 55 minutes	Servings: 2

INGREDIENTS

- 8 large carrots
- 3 tbsps. olive oil
- 1 tbsp. red wine vinegar
- 2 tbsps. packed fresh oregano leaves
- 1 tsp. smoked paprika
- ½ tsp. ground nutmeg
- 1 tbsps. vegan butter
- ⅓ c. salted pistachios, roasted
- salt and pepper

STEP 1
Set your oven to 450 degrees F.

STEP 2
Mix oregano, oil, nutmeg, paprika, carrots, salt, and pepper in a roasting pan.

STEP 3
Roast the mixture for about an hour or until carrots become tender.

STEP 4
Transfer to a plate.

STEP 5
Top with vinegar, butter, and top with pistachios before serving.

NUTRITIONAL INFORMATION
120 Calories, 3.5g Fats, 20g Net Carbs, and 2g Protein

SIZZLING VEGETARIAN FAJITAS

 Cooking Difficulty: 2/10	 Cooking Time: 120 minutes	 Servings: 8

INGREDIENTS

- 4 oz. diced green chilies
- 3 diced tomatoes
- 1 cored yellow bell pepper, sliced
- 1 cored red bell pepper, sliced
- 1 white onion, peeled and sliced
- ½ tsp. garlic powder
- ¼ tsp. salt
- 2 tsps. red chili powder
- 2 tsps. ground cumin
- ½ tsp. dried oregano
- 1 ½ tbsps. olive oil

STEP 1
Take a 6-quarts slow cooker, grease it with a non-stick cooking spray, and add all the ingredients.

STEP 2
Stir until it mixes properly and cover the top.

STEP 3
Plug in the slow cooker; adjust the cooking time to 2 hours and let it cook on the high heat setting or until cooks thoroughly.

STEP 4
Serve with tortillas.

NUTRITIONAL INFORMATION
Calories:220 Cal, Carbs:73g, Protein:12g, Fats:8g

GRILLED ZUCCHINI WITH TOMATO SALSA

 Cooking Difficulty: 3/10

 Cooking Time: 10 minutes

 Servings: 2

INGREDIENTS

- 2 zucchinis, sliced
- 1 tbsp. olive oil
- salt and pepper
- 1 c. tomatoes, chopped
- 1 tbsp. mint, chopped
- 1 tsp. red wine vinegar

STEP 1
Preheat your grill.

STEP 2
Coat the zucchini with oil and season with salt and pepper.

STEP 3
Grill for 4 minutes per side. Mix the remaining ingredients in a bowl.

STEP 4
Top the grilled zucchini with the minty salsa.

NUTRITIONAL INFORMATION
Calories 71, Fat 5 g, Carbs 6 g, Protein 2 g

BROCCOLI CREAM

 Cooking Difficulty:
3/10

 Cooking Time:
20 minutes

 Servings:
4

INGREDIENTS

- 1 lb. broccoli florets
- 4 c. vegetable stock
- 2 chopped shallots
- 1 tsp. chili powder
- salt
- black pepper
- 2 minced garlic cloves
- 2 tbsps. olive oil
- 1 tbsp. chopped dill

STEP 1
Heat up a pot with the oil over medium-high heat; add the shallots and the garlic and sauté for 2 minutes.

STEP 2
Add the broccoli and the other ingredients bring to a simmer then cook over medium heat for 18 minutes.

STEP 3
Blend the mix using an immersion blender, divide the cream into bowls and serve.

NUTRITIONAL INFORMATION
Calories 111, Fat 8g, Carbs 10.2g, Protein 3.7g

LINGUINE WITH WILD MUSHROOMS

Cooking Difficulty: 2/10	Cooking Time: 10 minutes	Servings: 4

INGREDIENTS

- 12 oz. mixed mushrooms, sliced
- 2 green onions, sliced
- 1 ½ tsps. minced garlic
- 1 lb. whole-grain linguine pasta, cooked
- ¼ c. nutritional yeast
- ½ tsp. salt
- ¾ tsp. ground black pepper
- 6 tbsps. olive oil
- ¾ c. vegetable stock, hot

STEP 1
Take a skillet pan, place it over medium-high heat, add garlic and mushroom and cook for 5 minutes until tender.

STEP 2
Transfer the vegetables to a pot, add pasta and remaining ingredients, except for green onions, toss until combined and cook for 3 minutes until hot.

STEP 3
Garnish with green onions and serve.

NUTRITIONAL INFORMATION
Calories: 430, Fat: 15 g, Carbs: 62 g, Protein: 15 g

LEEKS CREAM

 Cooking Difficulty: 3/10	Cooking Time: 30 minutes	Servings: 4

INGREDIENTS

- 4 sliced leeks
- 4 c. vegetable stock
- 1 tbsp. olive oil
- 2 chopped shallots
- 1 tbsp. chopped rosemary
- salt
- black pepper
- 1 c. heavy cream
- 1 tbsp. chopped chives

STEP 1

Heat up a pot with the oil over medium-high heat; add the shallots and the leeks and sauté for 5 minutes.

STEP 2

Add the stock and the other ingredients except the chives bring to a simmer then cook over medium heat for 25 minutes stirring from time to time.

STEP 3

Blend the soup using an immersion blender, ladle it into bowls, sprinkle the chives on top and serve.

NUTRITIONAL INFORMATION
Calories 150, Fat 3g, Carbs 2g, Protein 6g

EGGPLANT PARMESAN

 Cooking Difficulty: 3/10

 Cooking Time: 45 minutes

 Servings: 8

INGREDIENTS

- cooking spray
- 2 eggplants, sliced into rounds
- salt and pepper
- 2 tbsps. olive oil
- 1 c. onion, chopped
- 2 cloves garlic, crushed and minced
- 28 oz. crushed tomatoes
- ¼ c. red wine
- 1 tsp. dried basil
- 1 tsp. dried oregano
- ½ c. parmesan cheese
- 1 c. mozzarella cheese
- basil leaves, chopped

NUTRITIONAL INFORMATION
Calories 192, Fat 9 g, Carbs 16 g, Protein 10 g

STEP 1
Preheat your oven to 400 degrees f.

STEP 2
Spray your baking pan with oil.

STEP 3
Arrange the eggplant in the baking pan.

STEP 4
Season with salt and pepper. Roast for 20 minutes.

STEP 5
Over medium heat, set a pan in place. Add the oil and cook the onion for 4 minutes.

STEP 6
Add in garlic and cook for 2 more minutes.

STEP 7
Stir in the rest of the ingredients except the cheese and basil.

STEP 8
Simmer for 10 minutes.

STEP 9
Spread the sauce on a baking dish. Top with the eggplant slices.

STEP 10
Sprinkle the mozzarella and parmesan on top.

STEP 11
Bake in the oven for 25 minutes.

DESSERTS & SNACKS

YOGURT DIP

Cooking Difficulty: 2/10	Cooking Time: 7 minutes	Servings: 4

INGREDIENTS

- 1 mini cucumber
- 1 c. greek yogurt
- 4 spring onions
- 1 garlic clove
- 3 tbsps. chopped fresh mint
- salt
- black pepper
- sprigs of mint and dill, to garnish

STEP 1
Dice finely, the cucumber. Trim the spring onions and chop with garlic very finely.

STEP 2
Stir the yogurt until smooth; add in the cucumber, onions, garlic, and mint.

STEP 3
Add pepper and salt for seasoning and garnish with sprigs of mint and dill.

NUTRITIONAL INFORMATION
4 Calories, 0.2g Fats, 0.3g Net Carbs, and 0.3g Protein

PEANUT BUTTER POPCORN

 Cooking Difficulty: 3/10	Cooking Time: 12 minutes	Servings: 4

INGREDIENTS

- 2 tbsps. peanut oil
- ½ c. popcorn kernels
- ½ tsp. sea salt
- ⅓ c. peanut butter
- ¼ c. agave syrup
- ¼ c. honey

STEP 1
Combine popcorn kernels and peanut oil in a pot.

STEP 2
Over medium heat, shake the pot gently until all corn is popped.

STEP 3
In a saucepan, combine the honey and agave syrup. Cook over low heat for 5 min, then add the peanut butter and stir.

STEP 4
Coat the popcorn with prepared sauce.

NUTRITIONAL INFORMATION
430 Calories, 9g Protein, 20g Fat, 56g Carbs

SPICY CABBAGE

Cooking Difficulty: 3/10	Cooking Time: 40 minutes	Servings: 8

INGREDIENTS

- 1 medium size shredded red cabbage
- 1 tbsp. olive oil
- ½ c. chopped onions
- 1 tbsp. mustard seed
- 2 tsps. golden caster sugar
- 2 tsps. red wine vinegar
- 1 chopped ginger
- zest and juice of 1 orange

STEP 1

In a saucepan, heat oil and stir in onions, cabbage, ginger, and mustard seeds. Allow it to cook gently for about 5 minutes until softened.

STEP 2

Sprinkle over the sugar, continued with the vinegar and orange juice and zest. Cover the pan, cook the mixture over medium heat for 15 minutes, then reduce the heat and leave it uncovered to simmer for another 20 minutes.

NUTRITIONAL INFORMATION

82 Calories, 3g Fats, 10g Net Carbs, and 2g Protein

CRISPY BAKED APPLE

 Cooking Difficulty: 2/10	Cooking Time: 120 minutes	Servings: 2

INGREDIENTS

- 1 tsp. cinnamon sugar
- 2 apples

STEP 1

Pre-heat your oven to 200 degrees Fahrenheit.

STEP 2

Use a knife to carefully slice the apples thinly. Remove the seeds.

STEP 3

Use parchment paper in the baking sheet and arrange the apple slices make sure that it will not overlap each other.

STEP 4

Sprinkle cinnamon sugar on top of the apple.

STEP 5

Bake for one hour, then flip. Bake for another hour, flip occasionally until all the apple slices are dry.

NUTRITIONAL INFORMATION

35 Calories, 10g Carbs, 0g Protein, 0g Fat

MARINATED OLIVES

 Cooking Difficulty: 1/10	Cooking Time: 2 minutes	Servings: 8

INGREDIENTS

- 1 1/3 c. green or tan olives
- 4 tbsps. chopped coriander
- 4 tbsps. chopped flat leaf parsley
- 1 crushed garlic clove
- 1 tsp. grated ginger
- 1 sliced red chili
- ¼ lemon

STEP 1

Press the olives to break slightly, soak in cold water overnight, and then drain.

STEP 2

Mix well the ingredients and pour into the jars to marinade the olives. Place the jar in the fridge for at least 1 week, shaking 2-3 time.

NUTRITIONAL INFORMATION

404.7 Calories, 40.0g Fats, 13.1g Net Carbs, 0.5g Protein

BEETS CHIPS

 Cooking Difficulty: 2/10	Cooking Time: 37 minutes	Servings: 4

INGREDIENTS

- 1 tbsp. olive oil
- 2 tsps. garlic, minced
- 2 beets, peeled and thinly sliced
- 1 tsp. cumin, ground

STEP 1

Spread the beet chips on a lined baking sheet, add the oil and the other ingredients, toss, introduce in the oven and bake at 400 degrees F for 35 minutes.

STEP 2

Divide into bowls and serve as a snack.

NUTRITIONAL INFORMATION
Calories 32, Fat 0.7g, Carbs 6.1g, Protein 1.1g

FIGS WITH RICOTTA & WALNUTS

 Cooking Difficulty: 1/10

 Cooking Time: 3 minutes

 Servings: 3

INGREDIENTS

- 6 dried and halved figs
- ¼ c. ricotta cheese
- 12 halved walnut
- 1 tbsp. honey

STEP 1
In a skillet, toast walnuts for 2 min.

STEP 2
Top figs with cheese and walnuts.

STEP 3
Drizzle with honey.

NUTRITIONAL INFORMATION
142 Calories, 4g Protein, 8g Fat, 27g Carbs

APPLES AND YOGURT

 Cooking Difficulty: 2/10

 Cooking Time: 37 minutes

 Servings: 4

INGREDIENTS

- 1 c. yogurt
- 2 apples, cored, peeled and chopped
- 1 ½ c. oat milk
- 1 c. oats, steel cut
- ¼ c. maple syrup

STEP 1

In a pot, combine the oats with the milk and the other ingredients except the yogurt, toss, bring to a simmer and cook over medium-high heat for 15 minutes.

STEP 2

Divide the yogurt into bowls, divide the apples and oats mix on top and serve.

NUTRITIONAL INFORMATION
Calories 32, Fat 0.7g, Carbs 6.1g, Protein 1.1g

RASPBERRY PARFAIT

 Cooking Difficulty: 3/10	Cooking Time: 15 minutes	Servings: 2

NUTRITIONAL INFORMATION
Calories: 100, Fat: 1g, Carbs: 21g, Protein: 2g

INGREDIENTS

raspberry chia seeds
- 3 tbsps. chia seeds
- 1 c. frozen raspberries, reserve some for garnish
- ½ c. unsweetened almond milk
- ⅛ tsp. lemon juice
chocolate tapioca
- ⅛ c. seed tapioca
- 1 c. unsweetened almond milk
- 1 bar chopped dark chocolate, reserve some for garnish
- ½ tbsp. cocoa powder
- 1 c. water

STEP 1

For the raspberry chia seeds, put together raspberries, chia seeds, almond milk, and lemon juice. Mix until all ingredients are well combined. Make sure to mash berries. Cover with saran wrap. Place inside the fridge for 2 hours or until ready to use.

STEP 2

For the chocolate tapioca, put together tapioca, dark chocolate, almond milk, cocoa powder, and water.

STEP 3

Close the lid. Lock in place and make sure to seal the valve. Press the "pressure" button and cook for 8 minutes on high.

STEP 4

When the timer beeps, choose the quick pressure release. This would take 1–2 minutes. Remove the lid.

STEP 5

To serve, spoon an equal amount of chocolate tapioca in glasses. Put raspberry–chia mixture. Garnish with fresh raspberries and chocolate.

BROWNIE ENERGY BITES

 Cooking Difficulty: 2/10	Cooking Time: 7 minutes	Servings: 2

INGREDIENTS

- ½ c. walnuts
- 1 c. chopped Medjool dates
- ½ c. almonds
- 1/8 tsp. salt
- ½ c. shredded coconut flakes
- 1/3 c. and 2 tsps. cocoa powder, unsweetened

STEP 1
Using a food processor, set in walnuts and almonds to pulse for 3 minutes until the dough starts to come together.

STEP 2
Add remaining ingredients, reserving ¼ cup of coconut, and pulse for 2 minutes until incorporated.

STEP 3
Shape the mixture into balls, roll them in remaining coconut until coated, and refrigerate for 1 hour.

STEP 4
Serve straight away.

NUTRITIONAL INFORMATION
Calories: 174.6, Fat: 8.1 g, Carbs: 25.5 g, Protein: 4.1 g

PICKLED CUCUMBER SALAD

 Cooking Difficulty: 2/10	Cooking Time: 17 minutes	Servings: 2

INGREDIENTS

- 1 sliced cucumber
- ¼ c. rice wine vinegar
- 2 sliced onions
- 1 minced dill
- salt
- pepper

STEP 1

Put onions and sliced cucumber inside the Instant Pot Pressure Cooker. Pour white wine vinegar and dill. Season with sugar, salt, and pepper. Mix well.

STEP 2

Close the lid. Lock in place and make sure to seal the valve. Press the "manual" button and cook for 5 minutes on high.

STEP 3

When the timer beeps, choose the quick pressure release. This would take 1–2 minutes. Remove the lid.

STEP 4

Transfer mixture into a bowl. Refrigerate for 10 minutes before serving.

NUTRITIONAL INFORMATION

Calories: 67.5; Fat: 7.1g; Carbs: 16.9g; Protein: 1.3g

CONCLUSION

Healthy eating is a form of self-love and self-care. Being aware of the foods you are consuming is the first step towards taking control of your health, well-being, and your state of mind.

When it comes to diets, we all believe that it is something that makes us give up on the best foods, eat less, and count calories.

But, there is this pattern of eating, commonly known as the Mediterranean diet, which is somehow one of the best options for consuming fresh and whole-food rich in healthy fats, vitamins, minerals, fiber, carbs, and proteins.

Why is this diet so potent and powerful? The simple answer is because it is an eating pattern that keeps you full while providing your body with the healthiest nutrients your body needs.

This diet offers a wide plethora of foods such as fruits, vegetables, fish, seafood, nuts, healthy fats such as olive oil, and occasionally red meat, dairy products, and eggs.

Many people are afraid that they will not be able to follow it because they are meat-eaters, but the truth is, you are not forbidden to eat meat, only substitute it with fish (at least twice a week). Red meat is on the menu as well, but not as frequently.

Based on the eating habits of Mediterranean people (Italy, Spain, France, Greece, Morocco), this diet is a popular way of eating not only for weight loss but for excellent health and long life.

This means that a piece of fruit or vegetable, fish, leafy greens, legumes, and nuts are your first choice. These foods are not packed in unhealthy ingredients like it is the case with processed foods. Your digestion would improve, and your body would be able to start burning the fats, as you are going to eat only healthy nutrients.

When eating excessive amounts of carbs, unhealthy fats, and processed foods, your body tends to use the energy of carbs and sugars first. The fats are stored as reserved, which shows around your stomach, arms, and legs.

The moment you start eating healthy foods, your body would use the energy properly and would turn to its second-best source of energy, which is the fats.

Known for its health benefits such as keeping your heart in good health, this eating pattern would help you boost your immunity, will improve your skin, hair, and nails condition, and would lower the risk of severe illnesses such as Alzheimer's, type 2 diabetes and some cancers.

Studies show that this diet works miracles for people with depression and anxiety. Foods that grow under the sun are known to improve not only your general health but your mood as well. Your serotonin levels would increase just after a few days of consuming Mediterranean meals.

People love this diet because it does not require a lot of time in the kitchen and because you are allowed to eat as much as you want. There is no need for you to count calories unless you want to.

Prepare your weekly meal plan, purchase the groceries, and stick to the foods that are suitable for the Mediterranean diet. Your energy will increase, you will no longer feel lethargic, bloated, or in a bad moon. Your brain's cognitive functions and memory would also improve (this diet is known to reduce the risk in elderly people from Alzheimer's Disease and memory loss).

Your slimming would be easier, and you could keep your weight in balance in the long run.

Besides the many health benefits and the extended lifespan, the Mediterranean diet is an excellent choice for your budget and is environment friendly.

Finally, what matters is that you are healthy, content, and in a good mood.

I hope that you learned something new with this book and that it inspired you to consider the Mediterranean diet as your next eating pattern.

Eva Evans

Made in the USA
Monee, IL
05 January 2023

24581210R00111